for ing! £1-20

PORTALS

AJ DEANE

QUIRK HOUSE
Theatre Company

This collection first published in Great Britain in 2024
by QuirkHouse Books

Printed in England by Anglia Print Ltd, Beccles, Suffolk

ISBN: 978-1-3999-9453-8

A catalogue record for this book is available from the British Library.

About The Author

AJ is an actor, writer, singer, poet, director, public speaker, and co-founder of QuirkHouse Theatre Company, which specialises in showcasing East Anglian new writing and working with East Anglian talent.

The son of two Drama and English teachers, his love of languages, storytelling, and performing has been a lifelong passion.

He lives in Suffolk with his wife, two cats, and a lot of books. Not enough books, of course.

PORTALS

AJ DEANE

Other Works By The Author

SHORT STORIES & POETRY

Portals

Winter Tails

The Cats Who Caught a Cold

Too Hot for Dogs

ANTHOLOGIES (as contributor)

Journeys (Urban Pigs Press online)

From One Line: The Unseen Anthology

PLAYS FOR THEATRE

Highly Strung

(text and performance rights available from www.lazybeescripts.co.uk)

AUDIO BOOKS NARRATED BY AJ DEANE

The 'Utterly' Crime Series of novels by Pauline Manders

COMPUTER GAMES & ANIMATIONS VOICED BY AJ DEANE

Arma 3: Spearhead 1944 (Bohemia Interactive)

Card-en-Ciel (Inti Creates Co., Ltd)

Reynard City Chronicles (Polycomical)

Dedication

To my wife, Jackie

Whose unwavering support and belief made this book possible, whose presence enriches all who meet her, and without whom my journey would have been very different.

And probably much shorter.

Contents

Introduction

Let's start by confessing that this isn't your usual collection. Traditionally, there haven't been many writers who combine prose with poetry, and they are often taught as entirely separate forms. Where does that leave prose poems? Or particularly poetic prose? Or prose poems which feature heavy narrative?

First, let's discuss genre. The roots of Fantasy as a genre go back in some way or another for thousands of years; the lack of widespread writing education and the accompanying oral tradition of storytelling both naturally lend themselves to poetic forms as an easier way of remembering, and we've been discussing gods and monsters since time immemorial. For me, Fantasy remains one of the best ways that we have of exploring the human condition.

Science-Fiction is, of course, much more recent, and SF poetry, even more recent and more rare -

perhaps around a hundred years old - and it remains far less common today than its fantastical cousin. There are many notable names in this field, however (too many to list here!), most of whom I've read novels by, but not their SF poetry. I thought I was original, but there is nothing new under the (twin) sun(s)! More than a lifetime's worth of SFF poetry education awaits me. Perhaps they will perfect life *extension* in the meantime.

So, back to this collection. I am an often-overflowing ideas-fountain, but am far less often able to sit down and apply myself to writing a novel, or even short stories. My attention span and work as an actor rarely allow me to focus that way, and my laptop and several writing pads are stuffed with notes, interrupted first drafts, and tales which may as well have been put into suspended animation, or pricked by a spinning wheel.

As a poet and a storyteller at heart, however, what better way to channel the ideas in my head than to write shorter pieces and collect them here, in a portal behind a waterfall? If any of these become a springboard for someone else to take inspiration from, whether creatively or philosophically, then all to the good. It's a well which will never run dry.

I hope you enjoy reading these droplets from the ideas-fountain as much as I did writing them.

AJ Deane, Suffolk 2024

'Silvertongue'

"Words on pages!
Words for stages!
Fables told throughout the ages!
Tales of better worlds, and worse!
Words to bless and words to curse!
Tales to free or trap in cages!
Tales of warriors and mages!
Words in prose and words in verse!
Tales to tempt coin from your purse!"

hawking cry of the Ayjay 'Silvertongue' the bard

Neuronaut

(First published by Urban Pigs Press)

Pay bandwidth, n00b.
You don't just jack in and walk these pathways;
Can't take a pleasant stroll along the router routes
Or nice trips home to the motherboard.
No.
You go in unprepared,
You'll be cached out and on downtime
Before you can say 'gig',
Too bloatwared to dip those walls of fire.
Slackface and blockchopped.
You ping me?
Don't be blinded by the neon on the pave;
Stay no-face,
And keep your veed tight.
But you can goggle me hatting all you like –
It won't help you in the nowhere-everywhere.
You gotta deepdive and survive on your own.
Do your grind,

Prep your rig,
Jack in,
And sail those lightrails
Through the fizz-fabric of n-e-where.
It's a 'zing ride.
It takes strong circuits.
That's why I've got this 'gear in my head.
You'll need 'hancing, too.

Fingal Foke

Hark! With this tale we do admonish:
A lamp was found, a lamp was polished.
The hope was for a folklored genie,
Who would offer a wish times three.
From within the murky moke
Appeared the Mistmage Fingal Foke.
"In answer to your touch," said he,
"I have been summoned and set free!"
Then off he flew, a phantaroo,
To wreak his ruin on Tarazu;
The people of this thrice-damned world
Would witness his ire, now unfurled!
Eventually, the fiend most spurned
Was caught in spells, to brass returned.
Remember should you call his name:
First learn the way *he* plays the game.

Konrad’s Scales

I whispered my secret desire to the wind:
"I wish to become a god."
Curious gusts built to gales of laughter
But Boreas, he understood.
I would bring light to the darkness,
Shade the eye from sun's glare,
Temper vengeance with mercy,
Mete laws hard and fair;
Speak for the hated
And reason with love,
Counter doom-depths of Hades
With the Heavens above.
I offered Boreas my back,
And he pushed me forwards.

Is It a Long Way Down?

(First published in FromOneLine: The Unseen)

Is it a long way down?

About 43,000 miles.

Will we hit the moon?

The moon's more than 225,000 miles away.

Why is the sky blue?

Because the air molecules in the atmosphere
absorb mainly blue and violet light from the
sun, then radiates those across the sky. And
we just happen to see blue better than violet.

How big is the sky?

Which bit?

The at-mos-phere.

The atmosphere is made of many parts;
The troposphere is about eight miles; 'tropo'
means 'rotating'. It contains the ozone layer
and it causes most of the weather.
Then you have the tropopause.

The stratosphere is six to eleven miles above Earth; 'strato' means 'layer'.

Then there's the jet stream, or stratopause.

The mesosphere is twenty-two miles thick; 'meso' means 'middle'.

Then you have the mesopause.

The thermosphere is about three hundred and seventy miles thick; 'thermo' means 'heat'.

Then you have the thermopause, or exobase layer.

The exosphere is at least six thousand miles thick – almost as wide as Earth, itself; 'exo' means 'outer'.

It is pretty.

It is, from here on the AldISS, but thank the stars we're colonising outside the Sol system.

And 'sphere' is…'ball'?

Yes! Well done. We'll make a human of you, yet.

The Ares Corsairs

Beneath the bridge, they waited,
Ships silent among the stars;
Waited to prey on the trade convoy
On its way from Earth to Mars.
These moon-dwellers had been forgotten,
Left to rot on barren rock,
But soft colonists would tremble
When the Ares Corsairs ran amok.
The jumpgate with energy crackles,
And pirates their engines ignite;
Both Earthlings and Martians would come to regret
Ignoring the Demosians' plight…

The Gloaming Tower

The Gloom Knights stand a timeless watch.
Umbral guardians,
Cloaked in twilight,
Sentinels o'er the deaths of Kings.
Past those furnaced forms,
Dread path snakes deep into Darkwood.
At the forest's thorned heart,
Raised fist of The Gloaming Tower
Punches the stars;
Defies fair or foul, fiend or fey,
To dare essay its cold ramparts.
Those who resisted were broken,
Waves wracked upon a cliff,
Ground into the motte;
Devoured by barricades
Which grew ever-prouder.
Then the Gloom Knights appeared.
And the power of the Gloaming Tower
Was challenged no more.

Portals

There are doorways in the mist;
Ephemeral portals to real places
And other times.
The spirit Fabius tells me this is a nexus;
Points out the other doorways
Around the glade,
His spectral form bleeding ceaselessly
From the gladii of his unit's betrayal.

His men are darker shadows
But dare not approach me,
Full of real life as I am.
He raises an arm in farewell,
Turns away to confront his Forever.
I re-tie my walking boots,
Settle my rucksack on squared shoulders,
And choose a portal at random.

The Celestial Guide

I may encounter dead bodies,
But a Celestial Guide's role
Is too important to be forced from my path.
These fractured souls would be lost,
Doomed to eternally drift
As gleaming motes in the cosmos.
"Journey with me in love and curiosity,"
I invite these once-living
Specks of consciousness.
Most settle in my outstretched hand
And are enfolded to my heart;
We soar through creation to forever.
Some, too attached to flesh vessels once sailed,
Cling to skin sails and bone spars,
And are drowned by the void.

Time Keeper

It was not an easy door to open
But open it, I did.
He sat steering a great desk,
Marking passings in Time's Ledger.
He saw me and put down his quill.
"Pleased to make your acquaintance."
The god spoke softer than imagined.

Strangers

There are holes in the fence
Surrounding our world,
Put up in haste
To keep the Xenos out.
We thought our munitions platforms
Would be enough.
Yet how do you stop
Beings made of energy,
Which come from the hearts of stars?
Of course, we're all energy.
But not like this.
Not like *them*.

Isha Eurus

Isha Eurus rails outside,
Squalls enraged against the walls.
Beneath her ire,
Shutters chatter like oaken teeth;
Arthritic cross ribs creak.
Masters of a mastless vessel,
We huddle in hope
And candlelit whispers,
Lest her eye be drawn to us.
Weather this storm as we can.

Pussyfooting

We've managed to sneak ahead of them and can afford a rest, but we don't have long before we'll have to move again. Why am I even bothering to record this on my wristpad? I'll probably be dead before it's found.

Mrrlup's been really supportive. I know he's been quietly patching me up when I'm asleep, so that I think I'm stronger than I am. Purring me back to health. I don't know what I'd do if he wasn't here. But there's only so far we can get before they catch up with us.

Maybe he's slowing me down and I'd be better off without him?

Klaw's sake, that's unfair. Poor Mrrlup. I think.

He's sleeping right now. Dreaming, if his twitching tail is anything to go by. We've only got 15 clicks to the next Portal. Which is a shame, as this planet's kind of nice; temperate, one-gee, edible flora and fauna – the works.

But those things just don't stop. The Rats. They're eating everything, following us cross-world through our own Portals, chasing us back home to where it all started. They'll strip this world in no time. They're sure as hell not rats, of course, whatever they are. They just remind us of rats, with their nests and their numbers. Klaw, the *numbers*.

We're kind of lazy, my people, but sometimes that causes us to innovate a brilliant - and above all *easy* - solution. Hence the Portals. And the Rats. "Let's manufacture some things to 'pave the way' for us," we said two centuries ago; some bio-engineered lifeforms to 'get the job done' and build the Portals in preparation for our expansion. All very pro-active, productive, and piss-filled. Because while the Portals make travel between planets almost immediate, *someone* had to make planetfall and build the damn things first, didn't they? Had to land on some inhospitable Klaw-forsaken rock and do the hard work for us.

When Homeworld Portal lit up a month ago, announcing someone's arrival, we'd almost forgotten that travel was the gate's purpose. And through it stepped a Rat far more capable and well-spoken than the ones we'd sent out. He said that their work proceeded ahead of schedule and they were ready for us to take our rightful place in the galaxy. So we went.

And met wave after wave of them coming the other way.

Because during those accelerated generations' travel outwards among the stars, and away from us, the Rats grew in intelligence and awareness. They grew dissatisfied with dangerous work for so little reward. They grew angry.

Turns out, our 'rightful place' was oblivion - and the Rats' work was bringing it to pass.

I guess what I'm saying is: this is a record for another race to find, and learn from our mistakes.

Time to wake Mrrlup and get pussyfooting.

Justice

Dawn greeting slips stealthy
Between carrot-warted iron;
Dances soft on green-velveted stone
And across black-banded wood.
Bright beginning announcing shadows.
Pallet sighs forlorn as I sit
And clasp the blanket,
Each steaming breath
A knell of vain survival.

I drift for a time.

Am brought back by sounds outside
Of a darkly enthusiastic gathering;
Gossip and potato prices,
Parents shushing children
To stay quiet and watch.
It is the end.
The last day.

I sigh regret into the coverlet,
Saving breath's warmth for reasons unknown
To me or redemption.
A tray clatters through the trap and across flagstones.
I eat like a man condemned.

Nuke D.E.Z.

A century has passed since Boomsday.
Blasted Forest sighs under ashen skies;
Like us, it survives *Kumwotmay* -
Quiet, hidden, and disguised.
Two thirds of all life is now Unseen -
No riot of colour or birdsong here -
Soft we slip through the desperate-green,
As we hunt Albinodeer.
'Neath barren ground live my dear kin,
In the place where survivors were swept;
Our Nu K'dez, full of love and fear.
Forgive us. The Records Be Kept.
All around has not yet been laid waste
And though hope nowadays be reserved,
Is this the dawn of our new race?
Kumwotmay, We Must Deserve It.

Legacy

Rain rings plangent on iron and stone,
Steel and bone.
Smoke and cooked flesh
Lies acrid and heavy,
Among walls like broken teeth.
He coughs,
Fights bile,
Fights bloody mud pulling him down.
Genuflects before the ruin of his legacy.
Weeps.
Laughs.
He would bring this storm again.

Devas & Dreadnoughts

The outcome is uncertain.
Smolkin Danyil draws his sword
And threatens the beast.
He has little charisma but might intimidate.
He's done it before.
The die is cast; a one.
Naturally.
Danyil is eaten and the party scatters.
But something lucky happens.
Beast roars and bellows, shifts and stamps;
Its ribs are silhouetted from within.
In an explosion of incarnadine, visceral noise,
The beast ruptures.
From its corpse, Danyil rises,
Limned in light,
Rubies dripping from golden wings.

The Lady of the River

In patient moonlight,
The Lady of the River crouches
Beside the flowing years;
Dips graceful fingertips into Time's currents.
Next to her, a bridge of mossed stone
Spans the gently burbling waters.
She glances serene at silvered branches
And a fox snuffling curious on the opposite bank.
In earlier days,
- Though what is 'day' here? -
The Lady of the River would stand on that arch
And gaze downstream into history,
Feel the weight of the passing babble.
She rises,
Gathers her skirts,
And strides against the flow.
Into the future.

Rotations

Under the Glorious Three Suns™,
I lean on a rail, dockside,
And blow smoke plumes at the atmosfield,
Watching the *Rio Grande do Norte* pull away.
It brought tanwine from Bru'a,
Moonstones from Pixis,
And me, from Leezo.
This place has many names across Silveriver:
'Shaula' Lambda Sco. 'Taylate'. 'Gyrfalcon'.
But most people call it The Hub.
The biggest market in the galaxy.
Whatever you want can be found here,
For a price.
Bonewood from Carillion; diamonds from Tarsan III;
Fengroot extract and Mumble from Nesia;
In deep-hidden holds, slaves from Leezo.
I spit over the rail,
Saliva dribbling down the atmosfield
And into the filters, below.

The Leezans are meant to be slaves,

Some say.

I head to the bays to pick up my cargo.

They Arrived Under Cover of Rain

(First published in FromOneLine: The Unseen)

They arrived under cover of rain and darkness.

The guards on the ramparts of Salfort were hunkered down against the autumn night, paying more attention to staying warm and dry than what was happening beyond the walls and braziers. No movements were silhouetted against the fires and, apart from the pattering downpour, all was still.

Humans are so predictable. In their desires. In their selfishness.

The *softskins* had brought this on themselves. They came from the west in peace, they told us, they were no threat to the Urskin Tribes; they merely needed some little more land for farming, which we did not do, for crops we neither ate nor cared about.

We allowed it. Then the forts were raised. We protested but went unheeded. We have been a peaceful people for many generations, and we Ironpelts advised caution, but tensions rose.

The Black Claw Tribe were the first to fight back; they were dead in a fortnight. The Goldeyes are no more. Never again shall we hear the haggling of the Silvertooths or the poetry of the Brownfurs. The humans claimed territory after territory and we were pushed further and further east, until finally we were caught between the humans and... Well. More on the Others another time.

We attacked Haven, three miles away, a week ago. The Strongpaw Tribe led us in a charge of fury not seen in centuries, and we left it a smouldering shell. However, despite being *softskins*, the humans are numerous and we are few; too many of us were lost to attempt such an assault again. So, the night before Salfort, we squatted and planned in the Haven ruins, lighting no fires and staying out of sight, muffling our breaths to prevent steam plumes. Salfort was not large but it was important; it held the river and the humans' supply lines; its loss would be a great blow to them and boon to us.

The following night we marched, the tempest gradually building in front of us and masking our approach. We only hoped a Claw would be enough. A Claw is ten of us, a Paw is fifty, an Arm one hundred. No Tribe has ever numbered enough to need more. Unlike the humans.

The rain that night was brought about by magic. I had said I could not hold it for long; the war had been raging for some months by then, and I was fatigued. There were only two of us Stormsingers left, after all, and Greyface was busy supporting our struggle in the east. But the Elements had been easier to *Reach* than I thought. They were on our side in this.

As I stood on a low clifftop a quarter mile from Salfort, the wind ruffled my fur and rain sleeked down my pelt. I stared across the plain, paw raised, snout hairs twitching with my whispered incantations, maintaining the storm while the Claw cautiously approached the fort.

They arrived under cover of rain and darkness.

No alarum was called. No cries went up.

A Recovered Page from the Diaries of
Stormclaw Ironpelt

Legend

They needed a legend.

Long-tyrannized by a rapacious nepotocracy,
Downtrodden by lives made deliberately difficult,
They yearned for the comfort
Of freedom from want.
Some worshipped their oppressors.
Paid homage to Fame,
Corruption and Power,
Deception and Money,
Cruelty and Hypocrisy.
Their very own pantheon.
Yet,
Without even knowing it,
They, too, needed a legend.

There was one, age-old problem;
Not everyone recognises a legend
When she rises.

Self-Exiled

We know that dark'ning face.

In ire purpled,

Self-righteous eyes

Blaze with sneered malices;

Gravesome laugh 'scapes salt-crack'd lips,

In a bleat of vindicated woe.

We seek refuge on wreck-wracked shores.

The Lord evades the justice-sword

And we into exile go.

We Gathered at the End of Time

(First published in FromOneLine: The Unseen)

We gathered at the end of time.
Mistaken fools we had been,
Imprisoned by the same ill-begotten wish;
To live forever.
'Ever' is a long time.
All time.
Billions of years before the first stars formed,
In ebony nothingness,
We lived our vacant Spring of hope.
Untold generations of evolution,
Before the first hominids,
We lived our Summer of light-filled radiance.
Empires rose and empires fell,
And though one might last a thousand years,
It was but a grain in eternity's hourglass.
They thought us gods.
Everlasting.
Undying.

Unliving.

And then they, too, were gone.

Our Autumn decline, as planets died and stars

winked out.

And a long, long Winter of regret.

Again, we waited.

Until, finally, for the turning of the glass,

We gathered in weary and desperate desire.

At the end of time.

Shando L'anaar

They camped among the daggertrees.
Shielded by brush and twilight,
Marooned on an island of hope,
In a sea of blue-black grocklegrass.
Fire banked low as their urgent murmurs,
Ector's soft song and gentle lute
Accompanied Tefan's healing spells.
Yet Layne stirred not from her unconscious pain,
And Brahn's whetstone rasped
In time with her laboured breaths.
Alert for signs of pursuit,
Rissa patrolled the treeline,
Gauntleted hand creaking tight
On the grip of her impatient axe.
Shando L'anaar had been too powerful.
Too long had the necromancer festered
In the carcass of his church.
The party knew he would not let them go;
Would delight in adding them to his horde.

Rissa's grey eyes caught movement.
Grocklegrass whispered a warning
Through the stillness of fading light.
She called quietly over her shoulder; "To arms."
Layne's fate would be known by dawn.

Quite Human

The skycab lifted me away from my Block
And off towards the sparkling towers of uptown.
"You're dressed up. Off out for the night?"
Cab-bots are programmed to be quite human.
"Working. I'm a singer."
"I thought they were all 'grams, these days,
Or 'hanced. You don't look 'hanced."
"I'm a Nat."
I could never afford upgrades.
"You must be loaded!"
I paid my last 16 credits for this ride.
To go entertain offworlders,
Looking for something traditional;
Historic.
Archaic.
"No-one wants Nats any more."

Three Keys Hung on a Hook

(First published in FromOneLine: The Unseen)

Three keys hung on a hook
Next to the gaoler's chair.
Lifting them off, he almost left the third
Where it had been for twenty years.
One of steel, large and well-oiled,
Designed to open that first gate,
And all cells but the last,
With an orderly, dependable clunk.
One of brass, small and worn,
Which could have been for a desk or chest,
But its voice was a light click
Amongst the clink of manacle chains.
The one of black iron, heavy and rusted,
Had dustily clung to the hook.
It toiled in its lock with a skirling knell,
As it opened the oubliette.

Shadow

It moved through the night, unseen.
It preferred things that way.
Graceful and noiseless,
Keeping to the shadows,
It went about its task
With a singular mindfulness.
There.
On the other side of the road;
A female human, walking alone.
It felt the familiar pang of what it needed to do.
Soundlessly,
Stealthily,
It crossed the road and followed,
Briefly stopping behind trees
As carriages swished by.
Swifter now,
It moved closer.
Closer.
Close enough to almost touch.

And broke the neck of her would-be assaulter.

She heard nothing but the snap of a twig.

It dragged the man's body back into the bush.

And moved on through the night, unseen.

Terror-Form

The experiment was a success.
Life from barrenness;
Desert blossomed green and verdant
Into cool oases.
Some wildlife shunned this miragic miracle,
But not for long.
Such a realised dream shatters us humans
More than pragmatic fauna;
Leaves us bereft of hope
In an unreached aim.
One creature, however,
Despises this fecund abomination.
The Sandcur.
Its progeny would wage a future-long war
Against an invasion of water-life.

The King is Dead

"The King is dead!"
This I know.
Too long squatted he upon a throne usurped,
Reign ended by bolt from a killer never found.
In the tradition of my homeland,
The coronation-funeral proceeds slowly;
Stately, and obsolete.
Kaleidoscopic storm slashes through the windows.
From my rafter-high roost,
The coffin-shaped Phoenix flag flashes bright;
Pulsing sparks in a dark sea of grief and exultation.
"Long live King Tangir!"
The dead monarch's son, just eleven years old,
Stands between the throne and the casket.
He looks even smaller from up here.
And he is in much danger.
This I know.
Black leather creaking slightly despite the oil,
My gloved finger tightens on the crossbow trigger.

Venna's Invitation

When Venna fell our grief did spill;
A fading toll of hearth-oaths made.
We hardened hearts and fought on, still;
Yet hope was killed.
Betrayed.

So now we stand and pray for more:
The strength to feel afraid again;
That hour of steel play as before;
Our loyal watch remain.

Arise, arise!
Return to life!
Give thought of oaths left unfulfilled.
Return to love,
Pain, hope, and strife;
To blood-pulse now unstilled.

More tyrants live to overthrow –
Ears we shall open, and uncloud eyes.
Your second life you'll now outgrow –
Return to life. Arise.

Resurrection song by Sollsyng Reech

Cycles

The bar is busy, but I find a corner away from the crowd, the lights, and the band.

They're quite good, if a little Bohemian for me; 'grams on vocals and decks, a 'hanced Tyrossi girl with three arms on drums, a male Pixian on sax who looks Nat, despite the chip tattoos on his face, and a human lady on bass.

She is something else.

But then, she knows that.

Wearing earjacks, and sungoggles despite the gloom, she looks like she isn't paying attention to anything beyond the stage's footlasers. Of course, she somehow recognises me – even with the cheap 'guise collar I'm wearing projecting another face over my own.

I catch her eye and wait, nursing my drink until their set finishes and the place empties out a bit. She disappears into the latrines, so I grab a nearby booth table and pretend to study the menu.

She takes her time getting a drink and chatting to a few people before coming over, like she does. When she finally sits down opposite me she's flushed, and smiling like the Mona Lisa. The goggles hang around her neck and her gaze is intense, reflecting the lights in a way it shouldn't. She's plugged into some Clarity, I guess, probably to counteract the Mumble she'd jacked before performing. Sometimes, I hate how well I know her.

"Good set." I murmur, though it's not really to my tastes. She's aware.

"Thanks. Good face." She's blunt. "Successful trip?" She speaks a little too fast and too loud, enough for me to sneak a look around and lean forward before answering.

"Leezo's a dump. It's good to be back in civilisation."

"Yeah. With a cargo of slaves. Intelligent beings," her focus seems to ratchet up a notch, but she speaks quieter at my shushing gesture, "You've been gone a long time. Why are you here?"

"After this deal, I'll have enough to take us away. Away from the Trade and away from the chems. Anywhere you like." My heart and my hope are in her hands like so much brittleglass. And she knows it. I almost hold my breath. Almost.

"I like it here."

"It's killing you."

"There are worse ways to go. Like dying in a hold, from the third-rate stasis crate I'm in breaking down."

"They don't even know about it." We need to get off this. "We've both done things we shouldn't. But this would be a fresh start. A new planet. A new life."

She looks at me with her laser eyes for what seems like an eon, before answering. "You're wanted. For *slaving*. I know you've been gone for three cycles, but haven't you seen there's a reward out for you? We'd be on the run the whole time. I'm freer without you." When did she become so hard?

"I know someone who can help with IDs. Don't worry about that. Are you coming or not?" I try to be less caring and look away at the robot bartender wiping down the bar. "I'm going, regardless."

"I –"

A plasbeam hits her in the temple and she crashes to the floor, scattering our drinks. Glasses shatter unheard under the screams and shouts of fleeing customers. The shot came from the exit to the back alley and I see a shadow as it swishes out. It must have been meant for me. The reward. How did they see past the 'guise?

Mind reeling, I draw my plasgun and charge towards the back door, pushing my way through panicked punters.

I crash through the door.

And straight on to the raised barrel of a gun. The cloaked figure is just another shadow in the dimly-lit alley. I can barely tell what size they are, let alone a species. When they speak the voice is distorted, and I realise they're 'hanced with a vox.

"Trader of the Enslaved. Drop the gun. You have been found guilty of crimes against humanity. Your life is forfeit to the Galactic State."

I try to find the right words. Something. Anything which will get me out of this. I slowly put the gun on the ground and start talking, looking for a way to buy myself time.

"How can it be a crime against humanity? The Leezans aren't even human. It's no worse than cargoing cattle, or fengroot extract. Money's tight. You must know how it is. It's just business."

The figure reaches up with its free hand and pulls back the hood. I have to take a step back.

"You?! I just saw you die! How? Why?"

"You spoke to a 'gram. You're always interstellar; tech's come a long way since you were last part of civilisation. The reward'll come in handy when I leave this place. Alone." She smiles that Mona Lisa smile again, but her voice drips with venom as her finger tightens on the trigger. "It's just *business*."

If You Enjoyed This Book and Want To Know More About The Author

Follow Him on Social Media

Instagram: @ajdeaneactor

X: @aj_deane

Find Latest News on His Website

www.ajdeane.com

Read More on His Blog

www.ajpagefarer.wordpress.com